The Art of Courtship

How to find and maintain a loving relationship

ERIKA DECENA

COPYRIGHTS

edecena@gmail.com
Graphic design and production:
Erika Decena

ISBN: 9798375740454
Label: Independently published.

ABOUT THE AUTHOR OF THIS BOOK

The author of the book "*The Art of Courtship: How to find and maintain a loving relationship*" is Erika Decena. She was born and raised in a small town on the east coast of the United States, where she grew up surrounded by a large family and learned early on the importance of relationships and communication. After graduating from college with a degree in psychology, Erika began working as a couples therapist and specialized in helping people improve their romantic relationships.

During her career, Erika has worked with hundreds of couples and has helped many to overcome challenges and find happiness in their relationships. She has also written several articles and books on the subject, such as "Learning to Love" and "The Art of Courtship"; the latter considered an essential guide for those who wish to find and maintain a loving relationship.

In her spare time, Erika enjoys spending time with her husband and two children, traveling and practicing yoga. She is also an active charity advocate and devotes much of her free time to helping less fortunate people improve their lives and relationships. In summary, Erika Decena is a psychologist and writer with a wealth of knowledge on the subject of romantic relationships, and her book "The Art of Courtship" is an essential guide for anyone aspiring to find and maintain a healthy and lasting loving relationship.

Erika will remain committed to continuing to help people navigate the complexities of love and relationships.

TABLE OF CONTENTS

INTRODUCTION: Why is the art of courtship important?

Courtship is the process of meeting and courtship someone for the purpose of establishing a romantic and/or sexual relationship. It includes activities such as courtship, going out together, getting to know each other better, and establishing an emotional connection. Courtship is a stage prior to a committed relationship, such as marriage or living together, and can last from a few months to several years. Courtship is a way to explore a possible relationship with another person before committing to a long-term relationship.

During courtship, couples learn about each other's interests, goals and personalities, and decide whether or not they want to continue a committed relationship. However, not all courtship relationships necessarily end in marriage, cohabitation, or a long-term relationship; some may end in friendship or simply a temporary relationship.

A loving relationship is one of the most important things in many people's lives. However, finding and maintaining a healthy and balanced relationship can be a challenge. In this book, we will explore the art of courtship: how to find and maintain a loving relationship. Through practical examples and techniques, you will learn how to find the right partner, how to communicate effectively, and how to overcome challenges in a relationship.

Challenges to overcome in a courtship may include:

- **Communication**: Ensuring that both parties communicate clearly and effectively is essential to solving problems and building a strong relationship.

- **Conflict resolution**: All relationships have conflicts, the challenge is to learn to manage them in a healthy and constructive way.

- **Individual differences**: Accepting and respecting individual differences is important for building a harmonious relationship.

- **Change and evolution**: As both parties evolve and change, it is important to learn to adapt and evolve together.

- **Keeping the spark**: Keeping the passion and romance alive over time can be a challenge, but it is essential to maintaining a strong and healthy relationship.

- **Prioritize the relationship**: Making sure the relationship is a priority and devoting time and energy to strengthening it is important to its long-term success.

Courtship is not something that happens by chance, it is something that is built and nurtured. It is important to understand that courtship is a process, and that it requires effort and dedication to be successful. Learning the art of courtship will help you find and maintain a loving relationship that fills you with happiness and satisfaction.

In this book you will learn all about self-knowledge and how it relates to courtship. You will learn how to find the right partner, how to establish solid communication, how to resolve conflicts amicably, and how to keep the passion alive in a long-term relationship. Through the techniques and strategies shown in this book, you will be able to develop the essential skills needed to find and maintain a healthy and balanced love relationship.

Many of us are convinced that initiating and maintaining a relationship is a skill that can be learned, and this book will give you the tools and information you need to develop these skills and succeed in love. We hope this book will help you find and maintain a loving relationship that makes you feel happy and fulfilled.

CHAPTER 1: Self-knowledge in courtship

Self-knowledge is the process of knowing oneself; it is understanding our emotions, thoughts, behaviors, needs, desires, values, strengths and weaknesses. It is the process of understanding our personality, our mental and emotional patterns, our history and our goals. Self-knowledge also includes self-acceptance, both of our positive and negative traits. Self-knowledge is an ongoing process, and is also an important part of each person's personal and emotional growth. Self-knowledge helps us to make informed and rational decisions, helps us to build healthy relationships and to achieve our goals.

Self-knowledge is essential for courtship. If we do not know our needs, desires and limits, it is difficult to find someone who suits us and establish a healthy and balanced relationship.

In this chapter, we will explore how self-knowledge relates to courtship and how it can help us find and maintain a loving relationship. A high level of self-knowledge contributes positively to the success of a love relationship, as it allows us to:

- **Know your needs, desires and limits**: It is important to understand what you are looking for in a relationship and what you are not willing to tolerate. This will help you identify the characteristics and qualities you are looking for in a partner and set healthy boundaries in the relationship.

- **Understand your relationship patterns**: Many times, we attract people who fit into negative or toxic relationship patterns. By knowing these patterns, we can take steps to break them and attract healthier relationships.

- **Accept your flaws and strengths**: It is important to accept both your flaws and your strengths in order to find someone who accepts you as you are.

- **Identify your fears and insecurities**: Many times, our fears and insecurities can negatively affect our relationships. By knowing them, we can work on overcoming them and allow our relationships to develop in a healthier way.

As we can see, self-knowledge is fundamental to courtship, as it allows us to find someone who suits us and to establish healthy and balanced relationships. In this chapter, you will learn to know your needs, desires and limits, understand your relationship patterns, accept your flaws and strengths, and identify your fears and insecurities and work to overcome them.

1.1 Knowing your needs, desires and limits

Needs are the basic requirements that a person must satisfy in order to live a healthy and balanced life. These can include physical needs such as food, clothing and shelter, as well as emotional and psychological needs such as security, love and affection, a sense of belonging and self-esteem. Each person has a unique set of needs and it is important to recognize and work to meet them in order to live a full and satisfying life.

Knowing your needs, desires and limits is essential to courtship. It is important to understand what you are looking for in a relationship, what you are willing to give, what you intend to get in the other person, as well as what you are not willing to accept. This will help you identify the characteristics and qualities you are looking for in a partner, as well as assist you in establishing healthy boundaries in the relationship.

For example, if you are a person who values independence and personal space, it is important that you find someone who respects and supports those needs. Another example, if you are not willing to tolerate infidelity, it is necessary to establish that boundary early on in the relationship, before infidelity can eventually occur. By knowing your needs, desires and boundaries, you will be able to find someone who fits you and establish a healthy and balanced relationship from the beginning.

However, it is important to remember that needs, desires and boundaries can change over time, and it is important to be open to communication and flexibility in a relationship. As you learn more about yourself and your relationship, you may discover new needs and desires and may need to reevaluate your boundaries. Knowing your needs, desires and boundaries is an ongoing process that requires continuous self-reflection and communication.

1.2 Understanding your relationship patterns

A *behavior pattern* is a set of repetitive and specific behaviors and actions that a person adopts in a given situation or context. Behavioral patterns can be positive or negative, and can be influenced by internal factors, such as thoughts and emotions, or external factors, such as the environment and interpersonal relationships. These patterns can be difficult to change once they have become established, but with the help of a professional or through self-help, it is possible to identify them and work to change them.

Understanding your relationship patterns is an important aspect of self-awareness in courtship. Relationship patterns are the repetitive behaviors and attitudes we adopt in our romantic relationships, whether healthy or unhealthy. These patterns can be the result of our personal history, our previous experiences, and our beliefs and expectations about relationships.

It is important to understand your relationship patterns so that you can identify and change negative behaviors and attitudes that may be interfering with your ability to have healthy relationships. For example, if you realize that you have a pattern of choosing partners who do not value you or who control you, it is important to work on that pattern so that you can find someone who treats you with respect and values you as a person.

In addition, understanding your relationship patterns will also help you identify your relationship strengths and weaknesses, and develop skills and strategies to improve your relationship skills. This will help you build healthier relationships and find the right partner for you.

1.3 Accepting your faults and virtues

Defects are undesirable or negative characteristics or behaviors of a person. They can be physical or personality, and can negatively affect the relationship with others. On the other hand, virtues are positive or desirable characteristics or behaviors of a person. They can be moral or ethical in nature, and can improve the relationship with others. These virtues are considered a positive characteristic in a person.

Recognizing and accepting your faults and strengths is an important part of self-knowledge in courtship. Accepting your flaws means recognizing your limitations and weaknesses, and learning to live with them rather than trying to hide or deny them. Likewise, accepting your strengths means recognizing your qualities and abilities, and learning to value and trust yourself.

Accepting your faults and virtues will help you to be more honest with yourself and others, and to be more authentic in your relationships. By being honest with yourself and others, you will be able to build healthier and more genuine relationships. In addition, by accepting your faults and virtues, you will be more understanding and compassionate with yourself and others, as well as less critical of yourself and the people around you. All this will help you to be more patient and understanding, and to have less unrealistic expectations.

Accepting your faults and virtues will also help you find someone who accepts you as you are, and does not try to change you. Courtship is not about trying to change the other person; it is about accepting and loving the other person as they are, and the latter is very important to understand. If you learn to accept yourself, you are more likely to find someone who will accept you as well.

1.4 Identifying your fears and insecurities

Fears are negative emotions related to specific situations, people or events, which can cause anxiety or fear. For example, fear of heights, fear of enclosed spaces, fear of animals, etc. Insecurities are a feeling of lack of confidence in yourself, your abilities, your appearance, your intelligence, etc. These insecurities can manifest themselves as self-doubt, self-criticism, constant comparisons with others, etc. Often, insecurities are the result of past experiences or low self-esteem.

Identifying your fears and insecurities is an important part of self-awareness in courtship. Fears and insecurities are feelings that can negatively affect our romantic relationships, and can manifest themselves in a variety of ways, such as fear of rejection, insecurity in our appearance, or fear of commitment.

Identifying your fears and insecurities will help you understand why you behave a certain way in your relationships and how these feelings can negatively affect your relationships. Once you identify them, you can work on overcoming them and managing them in a healthier way.

In addition, by identifying your fears and insecurities, you will become more aware of your actions and reactions in your relationships; which will allow you to make more informed and rational decisions, thus avoiding falling into negative relationship patterns. It will also help you to be more honest with yourself and your partner, which is essential for building stable, healthy and lasting relationships.

In conclusion, self-knowledge is essential in courtship. Knowing your needs, desires and limits, understanding your relationship patterns, accepting your flaws and strengths, and identifying your fears and insecurities are fundamental steps to developing a healthy and lasting relationship. By knowing yourself, you will be able to make informed and objective decisions, and you will be able to avoid falling into toxic or negative relationship patterns. In addition, this will allow you to be more honest with yourself and your partner, which is fundamental to building healthy and lasting relationships.

In this chapter, we have touched on several important aspects of self-knowledge, but it is important to remember that this is an ongoing process that must be approached consistently and honestly with yourself. In the next chapters, we will continue to delve into topics related to courtship and how self-knowledge can help you find and maintain a loving relationship.

CHAPTER 2: Finding the right partner

In this chapter we will focus on how to use the concept of self-awareness seen in the previous chapter to find someone who is compatible with you. This chapter would include information on how to establish your criteria for a suitable partner, how to search for and find that person, and how to evaluate whether that person is really right for you.

First, we will discuss how to establish your criteria for a suitable partner. This would include how to identify your needs, desires and boundaries in a relationship, and how to use this information to establish what is really important to you in a partner. We will also discuss how to have a clear idea of what you want in a relationship, and how this can help you avoid falling into unhealthy relationships.

Secondly, we will look at how to search for and find someone who is compatible with you. Some tips will be provided on how to use social networking and courtship apps, as well as how to meet people in real life. We will also reflect on how to be realistic in your expectations and not settle for less than what you want.

Finally, we will talk about how to evaluate if someone is really right for you. In this regard, we will talk about some tools for assessing compatibility, how to ask important questions and have open and honest communication. We will also discuss how to be aware of your relationship patterns and how to make sure you don't fall into toxic relationships.

2.1 Establishing your criteria for a suitable partner

A *criterion* is a standard or principle used to judge or evaluate something. It can be a set of rules or principles used to determine the quality, truth or importance of something. Criteria can vary according to context and can be subjective or objective. For example, in a romantic relationship, the criteria may be communication, trust, compatibility, among others.

Before you start looking for a partner, it is important to be clear about what you are looking for. Establishing your criteria for a suitable partner will help you focus your search and avoid wasting time and energy on relationships that have no future. Some examples of criteria you can establish are: age, education, life goals, values, personality, etc.

Once you are clear about your criteria, it is important to be realistic and accept that no one is perfect. You may not find someone who meets all of your criteria one hundred percent, but that doesn't mean you can't have a healthy and happy relationship with that person. The important thing is to find someone with whom you have an emotional connection and with whom you can build a future together.

It is also important to keep in mind that the criteria you set may change over time. As you get to know yourself better and grow as a person, it is likely that your priorities will change and your criteria for a suitable partner will shift. It is important to be open to these changes and not close yourself off to new possibilities for love.

2.2 How to search for and find that person

Being proactive in finding a partner means taking the initiative to actively pursue a romantic relationship rather than waiting for a relationship to come to you. This can include going to social events, joining clubs or interest groups, using courtship apps or even asking someone out on a date with you. It's about being aware that you want to be in a relationship and taking steps to actually make that happen.

Once you have established your criteria for a suitable partner, it's important to be proactive and start actively looking for that person you want. This may involve going out more, meeting new people, signing up for online courtship sites or also asking friends or family to introduce you to someone. As we said, the important thing is to be proactive and not wait for the right person to eventually come to you; because they may never show up if you don't go out looking for them.

Once you meet someone you are interested in, it is important to keep an open mind and not judge the person prematurely. Take the time to get to know the person, talk to them, and find out if they really fit your criteria and if you have an emotional connection. Remember that you are also being evaluated by the other person, so try to be honest and sincere from the beginning. Facades, half-positions or ambiguities are, from the start, bad signs of personality that are almost never tolerated.

Don't be discouraged if you don't find the right person right away. The search for a partner can take time and is not always easy. The important thing is not to give up and keep looking. Also, it is important to remember that not all relationships are forever, and that there may be several relationships before you find the right person.

2.3 How to evaluate if that person is really right for you

Once you've found someone you're interested in, it's important to evaluate whether he or she is really right for you. This may involve asking the person questions, having honest and in-depth conversations, and spending time together to see how he or she behaves in different situations. It's important to pay attention to warning signs and things that make you feel uncomfortable or unsure.

It's critical to consider whether the person you're courtship shares your values and long-term goals. It's easy to be attracted to someone on a superficial level, but if you're not on the same page about important issues such as marriage, children, future or career, you're likely to face long-term problems.

It is also important to assess whether you have an emotional connection with that person. This means feeling comfortable and secure around her, and having open and honest communication. If you don't feel good emotionally in a relationship, it's likely that he or she is not the right person for you.

As a conclusion to this chapter, we can say that finding the right partner requires a combination of self-knowledge, clear criteria and an active search. It is important to know your needs, desires and limits, as well as to understand your relationship patterns. By establishing your criteria for a suitable partner and actively searching, you will give yourself the best chance of finding someone with whom you can build a loving and satisfying relationship. However, it is important to be selective according to your criteria, and to carefully evaluate whether the person you are courtship is really right for you, considering your values, long-term goals and your emotional connection.

CHAPTER 3: Communication in courtship

In this chapter we will focus on learning how effective communication is fundamental to building and maintaining a healthy love relationship. We will discuss the importance of communication in a couple's relationship and how it can help us avoid misunderstandings, conflicts and trust issues. We will also address how to learn to listen actively and how to express yourself clearly and respectfully, which is essential for effective communication.

Finally, we will discuss some specific techniques to improve communication in the relationship, how to establish regular times to talk about problems and establish desirable boundaries in communication. We will highlight the importance of learning how to manage conflict effectively, and how assertive communication can help resolve problems and conflicts peacefully.

The importance of effective communication in a love relationship and how, by practicing healthy communication skills, you can build a stronger and more lasting relationship can always be emphasized.

3.1 The importance of communication in a couple's relationship

Communication is the process by which information, ideas, thoughts and feelings are transmitted between two or more people. It can be verbal or nonverbal, conscious or unconscious, and can take different forms, such as spoken language, writing, gestures, facial expressions, etc. Communication is essential for building and maintaining healthy interpersonal relationships, including courtship. It is important to have good communication to resolve conflicts and understand each other.

Communication is a fundamental aspect of any couple's relationship, as it allows for emotional connection and mutual understanding. Without good communication, it is easy for misunderstandings and problems to arise that can erode the relationship. In addition, communication is essential to express your needs, desires and limits, as well as to listen and understand those of your partner.

Effective communication is also important for solving relationship problems and challenges, building trust, and maintaining a healthy and balanced relationship. It is important to keep in mind that communication is not only about talking, but also about actively listening and showing respect and empathy for your partner's perspective.

In summary, communication is an essential tool for building a healthy and lasting relationship. Learning to communicate effectively can help improve the relationship and avoid problems in the future. It is important to take the time to practice and hone your communication skills in order to have a happy and healthy relationship.

3.2 Learning to listen actively and express oneself clearly

Learning to listen actively is an essential skill for communication in a couple's relationship. Active listening means paying attention and asking questions to fully understand what the other person is saying. It also means avoiding interrupting and not assuming you know what the other person is thinking or feeling. By actively listening, you can make sure that you fully understand what your partner is saying and can respond appropriately.

Expressing yourself clearly and respectfully is also important in a couple's relationship. This means being aware of how you express yourself and how you communicate with your partner. Using respectful language, avoiding sarcasm and destructive criticism, and being aware of how your partner feels are some of the ways to express yourself clearly and respectfully. It is important to keep in mind that nonverbal communication is also of interest, and it is essential to be aware of how you are expressing yourself through body language and facial expression.

Expressing yourself clearly and respectfully, and listening actively, are key skills for communicating effectively in a couple's relationship. Taking the time to practice and perfect these skills can help avoid misunderstandings and conflicts, and improve communication in the relationship. It is important to remember that communication will always be an ongoing process; therefore, it requires effort and commitment from both parties.

3.3 Some techniques to improve communication in a relationship

As we have said, communication is key in any relationship, and courtship is no exception. One of the most effective techniques to improve communication in a relationship is "active listening". This means paying attention, not only to your partner's words, but also to his or her tone of voice and nonverbal language. By doing so, you can better understand their feelings and needs, and respond more appropriately to their requests and manifestations.

Another technique that can help improve communication in a relationship is the "4 R's rule": Recognize, Respect, Respond and Resolve. This involves recognizing when your partner is trying to communicate something, respecting their feelings and rationalizations, responding empathetically, and working together to resolve any problems or conflicts that may arise in the communication process.

In addition to active listening and the 4R rule, it is also important to learn to express yourself clearly and respectfully. This means avoiding judgment and blame, and instead using "I" instead of "you" to express your feelings. For example, instead of saying "you always make me feel bad," it is better to say "I feel hurt when..." This will help maintain an open and constructive dialogue. Some more common specific techniques to improve communication in a relationship are:

- **The "I" message technique** refers to an approach to communication in which the focus is on expressing one's own feelings, thoughts and needs, rather than blaming or accusing the other. The message begins with the word "I" to indicate that the speaker is talking about himself and not the other. The goal of this technique is to help people express their feelings clearly and directly, while avoiding accusation and defensiveness, which increases the chances of effective communication and a more satisfactory resolution. This technique is commonly used in therapy and personal relationships to improve communication and conflict resolution.

- **The "pause and plan" technique** for improving communication consists of taking a moment to pause before responding or reacting to something that has been said or done. During this time, you plan how you are going to respond or react, taking into account the feelings and needs of both parties, and looking for a solution that benefits both. This helps to avoid impulsive or harmful reactions and to improve communication, since you are responding consciously and considering the needs of both parties.

- **The "repeat and reflect" technique** consists of repeating back what the other person has said and reflecting your feelings and emotions. This helps to show that you are actively listening and understand what is being said. It also helps to clear up any misunderstandings and reassure the other person that they are being heard and understood. It is important to use this technique honestly and not to manipulate or control the conversation.

- **The "4R rule" technique** for improving communication consists of four steps: reflect, respond, relax and repair. *Reflect*: before responding, reflect on what is being said and how it is affecting you. *Respond*: respond honestly and directly, using "I" messages to express your thoughts and feelings. *Relax*: try to remain calm and avoid raising your voice or acting defensive. *Repair*: if there is a misunderstanding or any damage caused, look for a way to repair the situation and improve communication between both parties.

We can conclude this chapter by saying that communication is a crucial part of courtship and the development of a healthy relationship. It is important to learn to listen actively and to express oneself clearly and respectfully in order to understand and be understood by our partner. In addition, it is important to know and apply specific techniques to improve communication in a relationship; such as the "I" message technique, the "pause and plan" technique and the "repeat and reflect" technique. By practicing these techniques, the quality and effectiveness of communication in a couple's relationship can be significantly improved.

CHAPTER 4: Resolving courtship conflicts

In this chapter we will focus on learning how to effectively address and resolve disagreements and conflicts that arise in a couple's relationship. We will explore the importance of having a positive and constructive mindset when dealing with conflicts; which will include learning to see conflicts as opportunities to grow and strengthen the relationship rather than as threats.

We will also discuss some specific techniques for resolving conflicts effectively. This will include learning to identify and express your feelings and needs clearly, actively listening to your partner, and seeking solutions that are fair to both parties. Also, we will address topics such as the proper use of the "I" message, the importance of avoiding personal attacks, and how to remain calm and level-headed during an argument.

Finally, we will discuss how to prevent and manage recurring conflicts; this will also include learning how to identify problematic patterns of behavior and develop strategies to prevent them in the future.

4.1 Importance of being positive in dealing with conflicts

A *conflict* is a dispute or disagreement between two or more persons, groups or parties concerned with an issue. It can manifest itself at different levels, from a simple argument to a violent struggle, and can be caused by differences of opinion, interests, values or needs. Conflicts can be internal or external and can be resolved in a variety of ways, from negotiation to violence. It is important to learn how to manage conflict effectively in order to maintain healthy relationships and avoid harm to the people involved.

In any relationship, it is inevitable that conflicts will arise. However, how those conflicts are handled is what determines whether the relationship is strengthened or weakened. A positive and constructive mindset is essential to effective conflict resolution. This means having an open and receptive attitude toward your partner's perspective, and being willing to work together to find a mutually satisfactory solution. It also means avoiding attacking or blaming the other, rather than focusing on solving the problem. In addition to helping resolve conflicts effectively, having a positive and constructive mindset can also improve overall communication in the relationship. By avoiding attacking or blaming the other, it reduces tension and creates a safer environment for expressing thoughts and feelings. This allows both parties to feel heard and understood, which in turn can lead to greater relationship satisfaction.

In summary, having a positive and constructive mindset is critical to resolving conflict effectively in a couple's relationship. This not only helps to resolve problems, but can also improve communication and relationship satisfaction.

4.2 Specific techniques for effective conflict resolution

First, it is important to have a positive and constructive mindset when dealing with conflict. This means trying to understand the other person's perspective, maintaining an open dialogue and seeking solutions that benefit both parties.

An effective technique for resolving conflict is the "active listening" technique. This means paying attention to what the other person is saying, repeating back what has been said to make sure it is understood, and asking questions to get more information.

Another useful technique is the technique of "speaking from the "I". This means expressing your own feelings, needs and desires rather than accusing the other person. This helps keep the conversation focused on your own feelings and needs, rather than placing the responsibility on the other person.

4.3 Preventing and managing recurring conflicts

A recurring conflict is a problem or disagreement that occurs on a regular or consistent basis in a relationship, whether courtship or in a long-term relationship. It may be a problem related to communication, decision-making, time management, or roles and responsibilities in the relationship. These conflicts can be difficult to resolve as they often have deep roots and may be caused by underlying behavior patterns or problems. It is important to address and resolve these conflicts effectively to prevent them from negatively affecting the relationship in the long term.

First, it is critical to identify recurring areas of difference or disagreement in the relationship. Once identified, strategies can be put in place to prevent or manage those conflicts before they occur. For example, clear boundaries can be set or a code of conduct can be established to address those specific areas. It is also important to have open and honest communication about these issues and work together to find solutions.

In addition, it is important to learn to manage conflict constructively and avoid falling into toxic communication patterns, such as bullying or isolation. Learning to use conflict resolution techniques, such as active dialogue or mediation, can help prevent and manage recurring conflicts effectively.

Problem areas in a couple's relationship can be identified through observation of behavior patterns, recurring conflicts and lack of satisfaction in the relationship. It is important to pay attention to the feelings and needs of both partners and work together to find solutions. It can also be helpful to talk openly and honestly about any problems or concerns, and to seek professional help if necessary.

There are several techniques that can help manage recurring conflicts in a couple's relationship. Some of these include:

- **Pattern identification**: it is important to identify the patterns of behavior that are causing the recurring conflict. This will help to better understand the causes of the problem and to find a solution.

- **Effective communication**: communication is key to resolve recurring conflicts. It is necessary to learn to communicate clearly, honestly and respectfully in order to express our feelings and needs.

- **Acceptance and respect**: It is important to accept and respect our partner's differences of opinion and perspective. This will help prevent conflicts from becoming a recurring problem.

- **Negotiation**: it is important to learn to negotiate and reach a mutual agreement to resolve a recurring conflict. This will help prevent the problem from recurring in the future.

- **Ask for help**: If recurring conflicts become difficult to manage, it is advisable to seek help from a couple's therapist or counselor. They can provide additional tools and techniques to help resolve the problem.

In summary, preventing and managing recurring conflict in a relationship requires a positive and constructive mindset, identifying problem areas, establishing strategies to prevent conflict, communicating openly and honestly, and learning effective conflict resolution techniques. Managing recurring conflict is an ongoing process that always requires effort from both parties to maintain a healthy relationship.

As a conclusion of this chapter, we can highlight the importance of having skills to resolve conflicts in a romantic relationship. Negotiation, mediation, empathy, effective communication, etc. are some of the main skills that can help to deal with recurring conflicts. It is important to always have a positive and constructive attitude and to avoid being defensive as much as possible. An essential factor is to have self-knowledge, to know our weaknesses and strengths, and those of our partner, as this will help both to see problems from different perspectives and to find alternative solutions. We must learn to listen actively, communicate clearly and respectfully, and use specific techniques to resolve conflicts effectively.

CHAPTER 5: Keeping love alive

In this chapter we will learn how to maintain the spark of love in a long-term relationship. Once we have found the right partner and the initial conflicts have been overcome, it is important to constantly work together to strengthen the bond and keep the relationship healthy and happy.

A key aspect of maintaining love is investing time and effort into the relationship. This can include romantic activities such as dining together, traveling, or spending quality time together. It is also important to maintain open and honest communication, and to work together to overcome any problems that arise.

Another fundamental aspect is the ability to adapt and evolve together. Relationships change over time, and it is therefore necessary to be flexible and willing to change and grow together. This may also include learning to accept and love your partner as he or she is, rather than trying to change him or her.

Finally, it is crucial to keep the passion and romance in the relationship. This can include little things like leaving romantic notes or surprising your partner with unexpected details, or planning big adventures together. Maintaining passion is essential to keeping love alive and strong in a long-term relationship.

5.1 How to keep the spark of love alive

Maintaining the spark of love in a long-term couple's relationship is essential to ensuring the health and happiness of the relationship. One way to do this is through planning fun and exciting activities together, such as trips, get-togethers, sporting events or concerts. It is also important to take time to connect emotionally, whether through deep conversations or simply spending quality time together. In addition, it is important to show gratitude and appreciation for each other and to work together to continually improve as a couple.

Another way to maintain the spark of love is by investing in the relationship through couples therapy or working on projects together. Working together to overcome challenges and achieve common goals can strengthen the emotional bond between the two of you. It is also important not to forget the little things; such as romantic details, small gifts and surprises, as these can help remind you why you loved each other in the first place.

In summary, maintaining the spark of love in a long-term relationship requires conscious effort and dedication from both parties; this effort being shared, 50-50, and without imbalances.

5.2 Ability to adapt and evolve together as a couple

To evolve means to change and develop over time. In the context of relationships, evolving means growing and improving together as a couple. This can include learning communication and conflict resolution skills, developing a greater emotional connection, and setting long-term goals and objectives. It is important to evolve in order to maintain a healthy and lasting relationship.

The ability to adapt and evolve together in a relationship is crucial to keeping love alive. As people change and grow, it is important that the couple also adapts and evolves together. This means being willing to change and move forward together, rather than expecting the other person to change to suit your needs. It is important to work together to find new ways to connect and support each other as things change.

In addition, it is essential to be aware of the couple's individual needs and desires, so that they can work together to meet them. The couple should be open to new experiences and supportive of each other's interests and goals. Once a solid foundation of mutual support and accommodation is established, the relationship is more likely to be resilient to change and evolve in a positive way.

Ultimately, adapting and evolving together in a relationship requires compromise, solidarity and hard work. However, the effort is worth it, as it allows the couple to grow and strengthen together over time, which is essential to keep the love glowing.

5.3 Maintaining passion and romance in the relationship

Maintaining passion and romance in a couple's relationship is essential to keeping love alive. One way to do this is to plan regular, romantic dates, whether it's a romantic dinner at home or a romantic weekend away from the city. These activities are important to spend quality time with your partner and strengthen the emotional connection. Another way to keep the passion going is to practice surprise and improvisation, whether it's a small unexpected gift or a romantic surprise.

In addition, it is important to be aware of the other person's needs and desires and try to fulfill them. This can be as simple as making a cup of coffee for your partner in the morning or helping with a specific task. These small gestures can have a big impact on the relationship and help keep the passion and romance going.

Finally, it is important to remember that maintaining love and romance is an ongoing job and requires effort and commitment from both parties. It is necessary to be aware of this and work together to keep the flame of love and passion burning in the relationship.

To conclude this chapter, we can affirm that keeping love alive in a relationship will always require effort and commitment. It is important to remember that love is not something that just happens; it is built and cultivated day by day. Keeping the spark of love alive through small details and romantic gestures is essential to maintain the passion and romance in the relationship. In addition, the ability to adapt and evolve together as a couple is the key to overcoming challenges and moving forward together. It is essential to emphasize that love requires constant work and effort; but the effort will be worth it as long as we see how the relationship strengthens and grows.

CHAPTER 6: Practicing gratitude

In this chapter we will discuss the importance of practicing gratitude in courtship. Gratitude is the act of recognizing and appreciating the good times and good things your partner does for you. By practicing gratitude, you strengthen your relationship and increase your relationship satisfaction.

One of the first steps to practice gratitude in courtship is to be aware of the good things your partner does for you; this is very important, we must always recognize the effort and intention of the other for us. It can be something as simple as preparing a delicious dinner or helping you solve a problem. Often, these moments go unnoticed due to the daily routine. However, by paying attention to these actions, recognizing and appreciating them, you will be able to appreciate the effort and love your partner puts into the relationship.

Another important step in practicing gratitude in courtship is to express and communicate that gratitude to your partner. This can be through words or actions, but it is important that your partner knows that you are grateful for what he or she does. Not only will this strengthen the relationship, but it will also make your partner feel valued and appreciated.

In addition, it is important to remember that gratitude is not only about appreciating the good things your partner does for you, but also about accepting and appreciating the imperfections and flaws. No one is perfect, and it is important to accept and love your partner unconditionally. Practicing gratitude in courtship is essential to building a strong and lasting relationship over time.

6.1 Importance of practicing gratitude in courtship

Practicing gratitude in courtship is critical to cultivating a healthy and happy relationship. By expressing gratitude for your partner's efforts and contributions, you are building a solid foundation of trust and mutual respect. In addition, practicing gratitude can help increase levels of happiness and satisfaction in the relationship, as well as reduce stress levels and negativity.

Gratitude can also help improve communication in the relationship by fostering an atmosphere of appreciation and thankfulness. When you express gratitude for your partner's actions, you are giving a message that you value and appreciate their efforts. This can motivate the partner to continue making positive efforts in the relationship. On the other hand, a lack of gratitude can lead to resentment and a sense that you take your partner's actions for granted.

In addition, practicing gratitude can also help strengthen the emotional connection between both partners. By acknowledging and expressing gratitude for each other's small details and actions, you are showing that you are paying attention, that you appreciate and value the other person's efforts. This can help you feel closer emotionally and strengthen the bond between the two of you.

6.2 How to express gratitude to your partner

Expressing gratitude in a couple's relationship is essential to strengthen emotional bonds and improve communication. One way to express gratitude to your partner is through the use of words, either verbally or through notes or letters. You can tell your partner how much you appreciate his or her actions and efforts, and how this contributes to your well-being and happiness. Another approach is to show your gratitude through concrete actions, such as cooking their favorite dish or planning a romantic surprise.

In addition, it is also important to practice gratitude in difficult moments. Sometimes, it is easy to complain or criticize our partner, especially when we are going through a difficult time. However, if we put effort into remembering the things we are grateful for and expressing that gratitude, we can improve our perspective and strengthen our relationship. Practicing gratitude can also help us focus on the positive in the relationship and reduce tension and negativity.

Finally, it is important to remember that gratitude is an ongoing process and not an isolated or occasional event. It is essential to maintain an attitude of gratitude and look for opportunities to express it on a daily basis. This can help create an atmosphere of love and appreciation in the courtship, where both partners feel valued and loved.

In conclusion, practicing gratitude in courtship is critical to strengthening the relationship and cultivating a positive and grateful attitude in both partners. Learning to express gratitude to your partner sincerely and regularly can improve communication, increase relationship satisfaction and strengthen emotional bonds. In addition, practicing gratitude can also help you focus on the good in your relationship and appreciate what you have instead of focusing on what is missing.

CHAPTER 7: Learning to forgive

In this chapter we will discuss the strategies and attitudes necessary to learn to forgive in a couple's relationship. The ability to forgive is important to maintain a healthy and harmonious relationship. Without forgiveness, resentments and anger can build up and cause irreparable damage to the relationship.

Forgiveness does not mean forgetting what has happened or justifying the other person's hurtful behavior. Instead, it means releasing the resentment and anger you have toward the other person and choosing not to let the past negatively affect the present and future of the relationship; this is important. Learning to forgive can also help improve self-esteem and emotional and mental health.

There are various techniques and approaches to learning to forgive. This may include practicing meditation, reflection, dialogue, and teamwork with a counselor or therapist. It is important to remember that forgiveness is an ongoing process and may take time and effort. But in the end, forgiveness can help heal wounds and strengthen the relationship.

7.1 Importance of learning to forgive

Forgiveness is an emotional and cognitive process in which you decide to release resentment, resentment and hatred towards someone who has caused harm or made a mistake, and you choose to no longer hold that resentment or harbor resentment towards that person. Forgiveness does not necessarily mean forgetting what has happened, nor does it necessarily mean reconciliation with the person who has caused the harm; rather it is a way of releasing negative emotions and moving on.

Learning to forgive is essential for the emotional well-being and health of a couple's relationship. When we do not forgive, we hold grudges and resentment towards our partner, which can lead to a build-up of negative emotions, causing self-harm and contributing to increased chances of arguments and conflict. Forgiveness also helps to release the pain and sadness of the past, allowing us to move towards a more positive and healthy future. In addition, by forgiving, we are showing our partner that we value and love their relationship enough to overcome challenges and problems together.

7.2 Techniques and approaches for learning to forgive

One technique for learning to forgive is "active forgiveness". This involves taking conscious steps to let go of negative feelings toward the other person and focusing on the present and the future rather than the past. It is important to recognize that forgiveness is a process and can take time, and therefore requires patience with ourselves.

Another technique is "forgiveness in writing". This process involves writing a letter to the person you are forgiving, expressing your feelings and thoughts, but not sending it. This can help release pent-up feelings and find a sense of peace and resolution. In addition, it is important to learn to forgive oneself, as self-forgiveness is an important step in being able to forgive others.

In conclusion, learning how to forgive is very important for a healthy and lasting courtship. Forgiveness is a process that takes time and effort, but in the end, it can free both partners from the burden of resentment and bitterness. Learning to forgive does not mean justifying the offending behavior or forgetting what happened; rather, it means releasing control and anger toward that past incident. By practicing forgiveness, stronger and more solid relationships can be built. It is important to remember that forgiveness is not easy, but it is a valuable skill that can significantly improve the quality of your courtship.

CHAPTER 8: Prioritizing the relationship

We will discuss in this chapter the importance of prioritizing the relationship in courtship. Many couples face problems due to lack of dedication and attention to the relationship. It is important to remember that courtship requires continuous effort and commitment from both people to keep it healthy and strong.

One of the first steps in prioritizing the relationship is to set goals and objectives together as a couple. This can include short-, medium-, and long-term plans, as well as individual and team goals. It is important to work together to achieve these goals and support each other in the process of building a common future.

Another important aspect of prioritizing your relationship is spending quality time together. This can include regular dates, trips together, and quality time without distractions such as cell phones or televisions. It is also important to have individual time and respect each other's personal space, but it is equally important to maintain a balance and spend enough time together to strengthen the relationship.

Prioritizing the relationship is essential to maintaining a healthy and lasting courtship. This includes setting goals and objectives together, dedicating quality time and working together to achieve those goals, and maintaining a balance of time together and individual time.

8.1 Importance of prioritizing the relationship

The importance of prioritizing the relationship lies in the fact that, like everything else in life, a relationship takes time and effort to thrive. Without prioritization, it is easy for the relationship to fade and become simply routine. It is important to remember that a relationship is a commitment between two people and it is necessary to dedicate time and effort to keep it healthy and happy. Prioritizing the relationship also means putting it first in times of crisis or difficulty, rather than simply taking it for granted and hoping that everything will work itself out.

8.2 Steps to follow to prioritize the relationship

The following are the steps to follow to prioritize a love relationship:

- **Set goals and objectives together**: It is important that you are both in the same context regarding what you want to achieve in the relationship. Setting goals and objectives together allows you to work together to achieve them and move forward in the same direction.

- **Make time for the relationship**: It is important to dedicate quality time to the relationship to strengthen the bond and maintain the connection. Establishing a regular date or quality time can help prioritize the relationship.

- **Problem solving together**: It is important to work together to resolve problems and conflicts that arise in the relationship. This will help you both feel heard and understood, and find solutions that work for both of you.

- **Appreciate and value your partner**: It is important to show appreciation and value your partner on a regular basis. This can include little things like saying "I love you" or making a loving gesture, or big things like planning a romantic weekend.

- **Practice open and honest communication**: It is important to have open and honest communication so that you can talk about anything that comes up in the relationship. This allows both of you to be aware of each other's feelings and needs, and helps to avoid misunderstandings.

In conclusion, prioritizing the relationship is critical to maintaining a healthy long-term courtship. It is important to set priorities in life and make sure that the relationship is at the top of the list. This involves dedicating time and effort to strengthening the relationship, setting goals and objectives together, and working together to overcome challenges and conflicts that may arise. It is important to remember that prioritizing the relationship does not mean neglecting other important aspects of life, but rather finding the right balance between all the important areas. By prioritizing the relationship and working together, lasting and meaningful relationships can be built.

CHAPTER 9: Building a future together

We will finally discuss in this chapter how to build a future together as a couple. Topics such as planning goals and objectives as a couple, strengthening trust in the long-term relationship, facing challenges and overcoming obstacles together, maintaining emotional connection and intimacy as we age together, imagining and preparing for the future to stay together, such as marriage and family, will be addressed. Practical tools and tips will be provided to help couples work together to build a strong and lasting future.

9.1 How to build a future together as a couple

The future is the time that has not yet occurred, after the present. It can refer to a specific period of time or to an abstract idea of what has not yet happened, and can be considered from both a scientific and philosophical point of view. Generally speaking, the future is the place where events or changes are expected to occur.

Building a future together as a couple requires commitment and planning. It is important to have open and honest conversations about what you each hope and want for your future, both individually and as a couple. This may include discussions about short- and long-term goals, plans for life together, and major decisions, such as having children or buying a home or other assets. It is important to actively listen and respect each other's perspectives and desires, while working as a team to find a balance and a plan that works for both of you.

In addition to planning, it is important to work on strengthening trust and connection in the relationship. As you build a future together, it is critical to maintain a sense of adventure and excitement in the relationship while facing challenges and problems together. It is also essential to continue to cultivate open communication and effective conflict resolution to ensure a strong, balanced and long-lasting relationship.

Finally, it is important to remember that building a future together is a constantly evolving process that requires patience and perseverance. It is necessary to always be open to change, and to adapt together as life and circumstances change. With commitment, planning and a positive mindset, you can build a future together filled with love and happiness.

9.2 Planning goals and objectives as a couple

Planning goals and objectives as a couple is essential to building a future together. It is important that both partners are committed and work together to achieve their goals. By sitting down and discussing your individual and couple goals and objectives, you can find areas of common interest and work as a team to achieve them. This can include financial goals, career goals, travel goals, family goals, and more. It is important to make sure that both partners are willing to sacrifice and compromise to achieve these goals together.

Planning goals and objectives also helps to maintain focus and motivation in the couple. As you reach goals and objectives together, you can feel a sense of accomplishment and satisfaction; which helps strengthen the bond between both partners. In addition, by having a plan and goals in place, it is easier to face and overcome challenges that arise in the relationship.

In summary, planning goals and objectives as a couple is essential to building a future together. It is important that both partners are committed and work together to achieve their goals. By having a plan and established objectives, it is easier to face and overcome the challenges that arise in the relationship; all of which will contribute to strengthening the bond between both partners.

9.3 Tools for building a solid and durable future

Building a future together as a couple requires great communication and mutual commitment. It is important to have a shared vision of the future and work together to achieve those goals. This can include things like planning a life together, having children, buying a house, traveling, creating a business together, among others.

Planning goals and objectives as a couple is essential to building a solid and lasting future. This may include setting short, medium and long-term goals. It is important that these goals and objectives are specific, measurable, attainable, relevant and have a time limit for achieving them. These goals can be either individual or team goals, but it is important that both are committed and work together to achieve them.

To build a strong and lasting future, it is important to have tools and strategies to handle challenges and difficulties that may arise. This may include learning to manage stress and anxiety, developing conflict resolution skills, learning to forgive, having an optimistic and positive mindset, and maintaining a strong emotional and physical connection with the other person.

It can also be helpful to have the support of a therapist or counselor to help navigate the challenges of building a future, such as stress and anxiety, and thus maintain a healthy perspective. There are several techniques for managing stress and anxiety; some of the most common include:

- **Physical exercise**: Exercise is an excellent way to release accumulated tension in the body and reduce stress.

- **Meditation and yoga**: These practices help calm the mind and reduce anxiety.

- **Deep breathing**: Deep breathing is a simple but effective technique to reduce anxiety.

- **Relaxation techniques**: Progressive relaxation, guided imagery and massage are some techniques that help reduce stress and anxiety.

- **Talk to someone**: Sometimes talking to a friend or mental health professional can help release emotions and process difficult thoughts.

- **Set realistic goals**: Setting achievable and realistic goals and working toward them can help reduce stress and anxiety by providing a sense of accomplishment and purpose.

It is important to mention that these techniques are just general suggestions; and it is therefore advisable to seek help from a mental health professional if you feel that stress or anxiety is a problem for you or your partner.

To conclude, we can say that building a future together as a couple requires a conscious effort and mutual commitment. It is important to have tools and resources to face challenges and overcome obstacles that may arise along the way. With a positive approach and a continuous growth mindset, you can build a solid and lasting future with your partner.

CONCLUSION AND FINAL THOUGHTS

A determining conclusion of this book is that finding and maintaining a loving relationship is a constantly evolving process. It is important to keep in mind that there are no magic formulas for success in love, but rather it is a process of constant learning and mutual commitment.

First of all, it is essential to find the right partner by understanding yourself, what you are looking for in a relationship and the importance of having healthy and clear communication all the time. It is essential to work on resolving conflicts constructively and to learn to forgive and adapt together to keep the spark of love.

Second, the practice of gratitude and the ability to prioritize the relationship is crucial. Learning to appreciate and express gratitude towards our partner, and working together to put the relationship first, are key to strengthening and maintaining a healthy and loving relationship.

In summary, the art of courtship is a constant process of learning and mutual commitment. It requires effort, patience, clear communication, trust, gratitude, adaptability, and a positive and constructive mindset to face the challenges that arise. With these principles and techniques, a lasting and satisfying courtship relationship can be achieved.

www.ingramcontent.com/pod-product-compliance
Lightning Source LLC
LaVergne TN
LVHW052109160826
845678LV00015B/3453

* 9 7 9 8 3 7 5 7 4 0 4 5 4 *